The Wheels
The Friendship Race
Die Räder
Das Freundschaftsrennen

Inna Nusinsky

Illustrations by Michael Jay Roque
Illustrationen von Michael Jay Roque

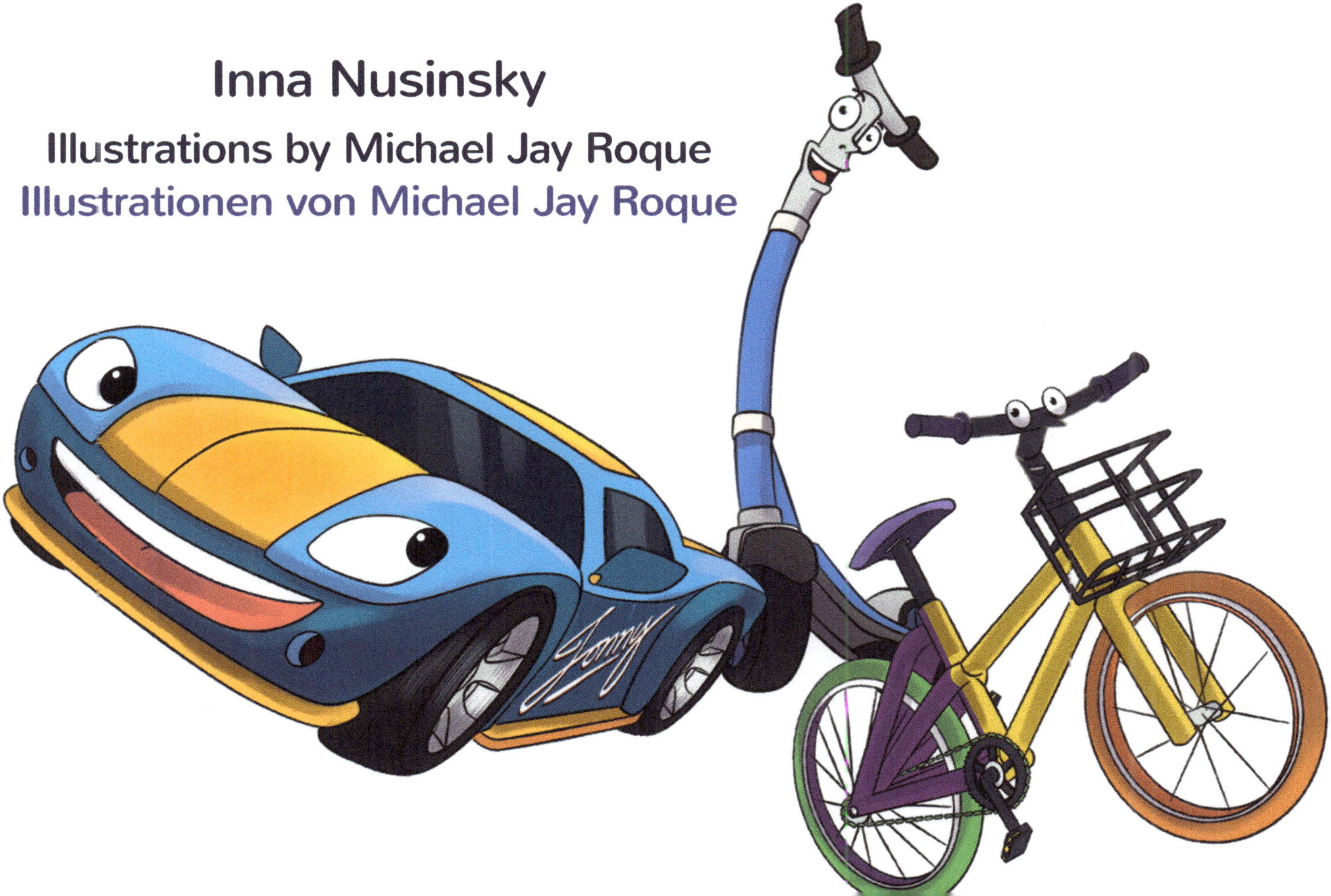

www.sachildrensbooks.com
Copyright©2015 by S.A. Publishing
innans@gmail.com

All rights reserved. No part of this book may be reproduced in any form or by any electronic or mechanical means, including information storage and retrieval systems, without written permission from the publisher or author, except in the case of a reviewer, who may quote brief passages embodied in critical articles or in a review.
Alle Rechte vorbehalten. Kein Teil dieses Buches darf in irgendeiner Form oder durch irgendwelche elektronischen oder mechanischen Mitteln, einschließlich Informationen Regalbediengeräte schriftlich beim Verlag, mit Ausnahme von einem Rezensenten, kurze Passagen in einer Bewertung zitieren darf reproduziert, ohne Erlaubnis.

First edition, 2016
Translated from English by Tess Parthum
Aus dem Englischen übersetzt von Tess Parthum

The Wheels: The Friendship race (German Bilingual Edition)
ISBN: 978-1-77268-958-7 paperback
ISBN: 978-1-77268-959-4 hardcover
ISBN: 978-1-77268-957-0 eBook

Although the author and the publisher have made every effort to ensure the accuracy and completeness of information contained in this book, we assume no responsibility for errors, inaccuracies, omission, inconsistency, or consequences from such information.
Please note that the German and English versions of the story have been written to be as close as possible. However, in some cases they differ in order to accommodate nuances and fluidity of each language.

Jonny the car looked at himself in the shop window. How handsome he was! And what speed – he could beat even race cars!

Jonny, das Auto, sah sich im Schaufenster an. Wie hübsch er doch war! Und wie schnell – er konnte sogar Rennwagen schlagen!

"I'm the pride of the neighborhood," he yelled.

„Ich bin der Stolz der Nachbarschaft!", rief er.

Just then, two braking sounds broke his daydream.

Genau in diesem Moment unterbrachen zwei Bremsgeräusche seinen Tagtraum.

Suddenly, he saw them reflected in the glass window – his friends Mike the bike and Scott the scooter.

Plötzlich sah er ihr Spiegelbild im Glasfenster – seine Freunde Mike, das Fahrrad, und Scott, den Roller.

"Hey Jonny!" his friends said. "What's up?"

„Hey Jonny!" sagten seine Freunde. „Was gibt's?"

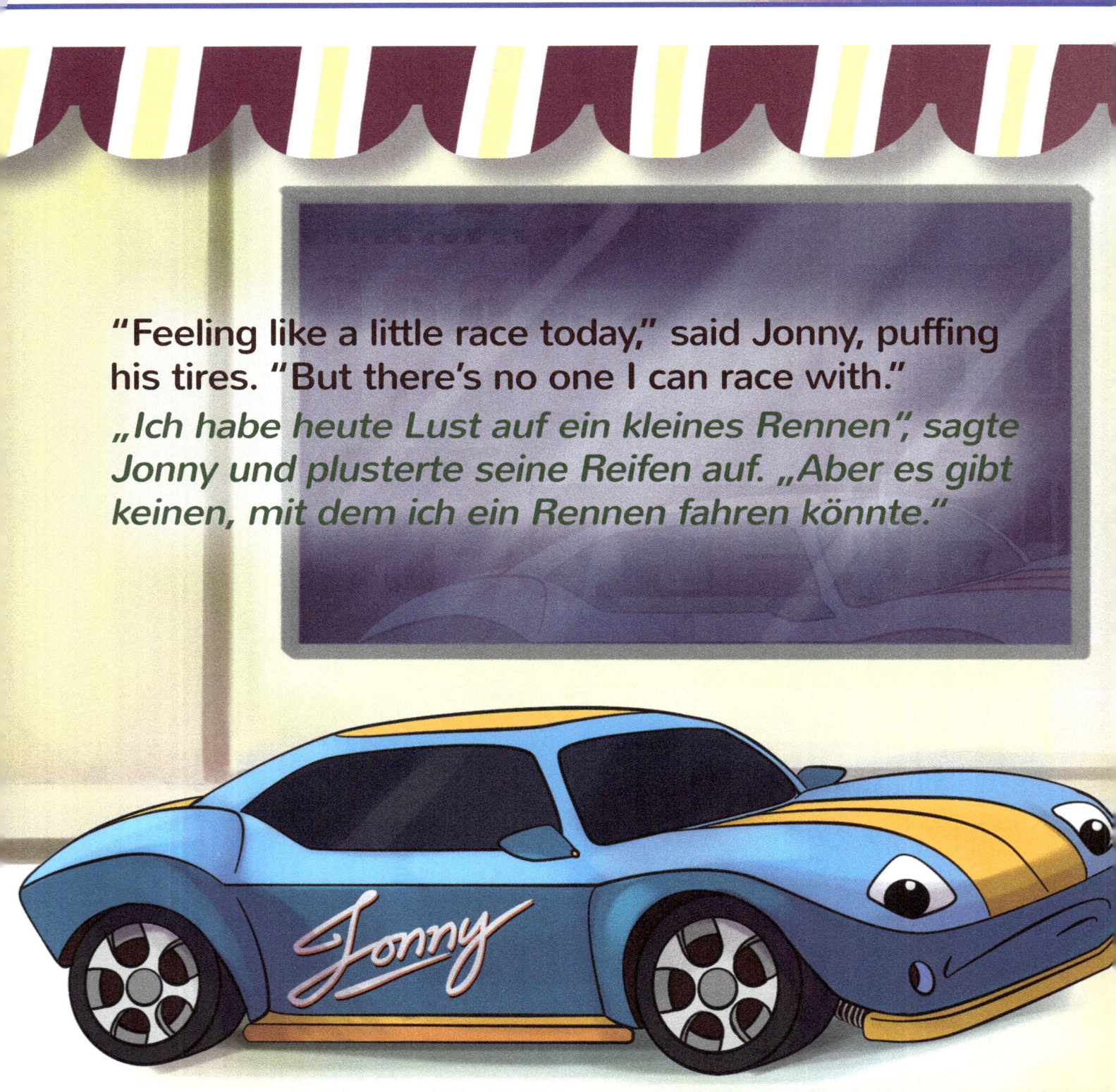

"Feeling like a little race today," said Jonny, puffing his tires. "But there's no one I can race with."

„Ich habe heute Lust auf ein kleines Rennen", sagte Jonny und plusterte seine Reifen auf. „Aber es gibt keinen, mit dem ich ein Rennen fahren könnte."

"We can race with you!" said Mike with excitement.
„Wir können ein Rennen mit dir fahren!", sagte Mike aufgeregt.

"That's what friends are for!" added Scott.
„Dafür sind Freunde da!", fügte Scott hinzu.

Jonny didn't show much enthusiasm. "Mmm... A champion needs an equal to compete with."
Jonny zeigte nicht viel Begeisterung. „Hmmm... Ein Champion braucht einen ebenbürtigen Gegner, mit dem er sich messen kann."

Mike and Scott looked at each other. A cloud passed over their faces.

Mike und Scott sahen einander an. Ihre Gesichter wurden trüb.

"Are we not good?" asked Mike.

„Sind wir nicht gut?", fragte Mike.

"Oh, you're good," Jonny made a face in the glass window. "But not good enough."

„Oh, ihr seid gut." Jonny schnitt eine Grimasse im Glasfenster. „Aber nicht gut

"Okay, Jonny," said Scott. "We challenge you to a race right now! Let's do Hill Road and see who finishes first."

„Ok, Jonny", sagte Scott. „Wir fordern dich jetzt sofort zu einem Rennen heraus! Lass uns die Hügelstraße hinauf fahren und schauen, wer zuerst ankommt."

Jonny considered it with a smirk.

Jonny überlegte es sich grinsend.

As they reached Hill Road, the race began.
Als sie die Hill Road erreichten, begann das Rennen.

It started with a steep climb. Jonny roared and in seconds was over the incline.
Es fing mit einem steilen Anstieg an. Jonny dröhnte und schaffte es in Sekunden über die Steigung.

Mike the bike was already half way... But poor Scott the scooter was huffing and puffing, slowly climbing up.
Mike, das Fahrrad, war schon auf halbem Wege... Doch der arme Roller Scott schnaufte und keuchte, während er langsam hinauffuhr.

Jonny reached the hill and stopped. He looked at the rearview mirror – his friends were far behind.

Jonny erreichte den Hügel und hielt an. Er schaute in den Rückspiegel – seine Freunde lagen weit zurück.

He was bored. At least the music on the radio was good! He closed his eyes and started moving to the beat.

Er war gelangweilt. Zumindest die Musik im Radio war gut! Er schloss seine Augen und fing an, sich im Takt zu bewegen.

Suddenly, something whirred past him. There was only smoke. Mike?

Plötzlich sauste etwas an ihm vorbei. Da war nur Rauch.

Before he could say a word something else went by. Jonny looked through the disappearing smoke—that was Scott racing ahead!

Bevor er ein Wort sagen konnte, fuhr etwas anderes vorbei. Jonny schaute durch den verschwindenden Rauch—das war Scott, der voraus brauste!

No way! Now he panicked. He should win!

Auf keinen Fall! Nun bekam er Panik. Er sollte gewinnen!

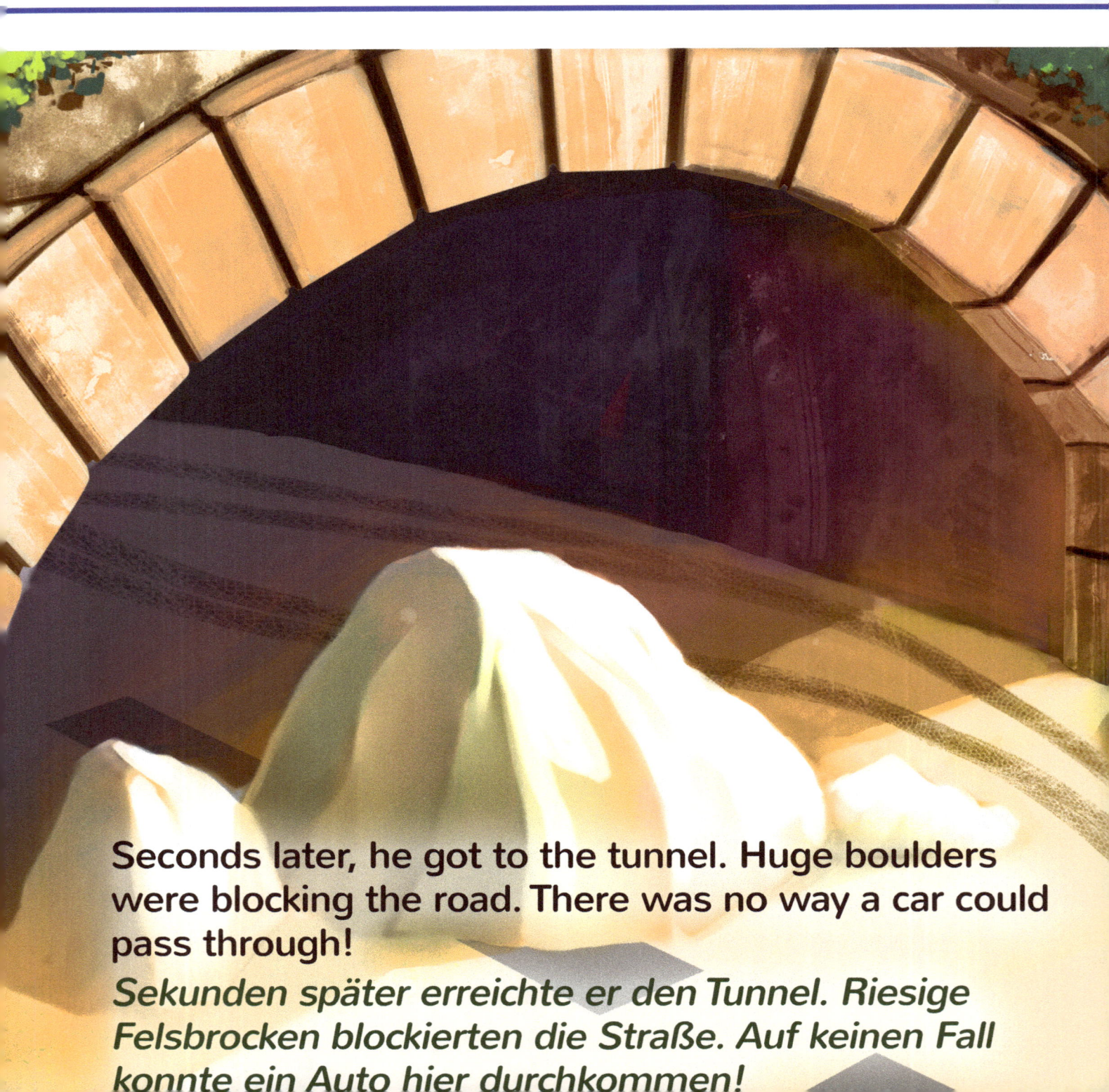

Seconds later, he got to the tunnel. Huge boulders were blocking the road. There was no way a car could pass through!

Sekunden später erreichte er den Tunnel. Riesige Felsbrocken blockierten die Straße. Auf keinen Fall konnte ein Auto hier durchkommen!

But then, he saw the tire marks of both Mike and Scott. They had negotiated their way around the stone boulders! Jonny sighed.

Doch dann sah er die Reifenspuren von Mike und Scott. Sie hatten sich ihren Weg um die Gesteinsbrocken herum gebahnt. Jonny seufzte.

Meanwhile, Mike came out on the other side of the tunnel. He was leading.

In der Zwischenzeit kam Mike auf der anderen Seite des Tunnels heraus. Er lag in Führung.

What kind of a win is that when your friends lose? he thought.
Was für ein Sieg ist das, wenn deine Freunde verlieren?, dachte er.

In seconds, Scott was next to him.
Innerhalb von Sekunden war Scott neben ihm.

"Why did you stop, Mike?" he asked. "You could've won the race!"
„Warum hast du angehalten, Mike?", fragte er. „Du hättest das Rennen gewinnen können!"

"Yeah but...Jonny could be stuck back there..." said Mike, looking towards the tunnel.
„Ja, aber... Jonny könnte dort hinten feststecken...", sagte Mike und schaute Richtung Tunnel.

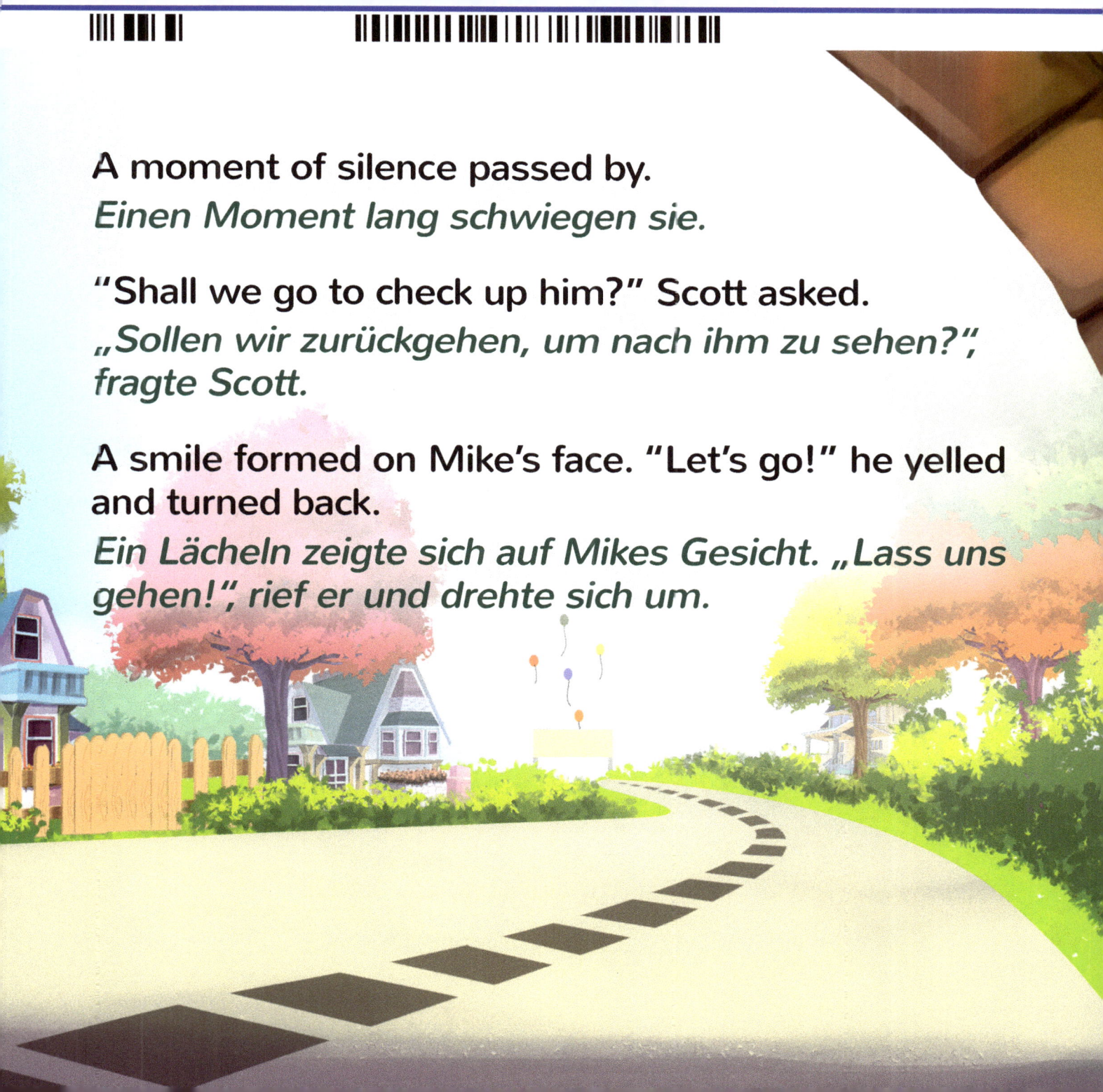

A moment of silence passed by.
Einen Moment lang schwiegen sie.

"Shall we go to check up him?" Scott asked.
„Sollen wir zurückgehen, um nach ihm zu sehen?", fragte Scott.

A smile formed on Mike's face. "Let's go!" he yelled and turned back.
Ein Lächeln zeigte sich auf Mikes Gesicht. „Lass uns gehen!", rief er und drehte sich um.

At the blocked tunnel, Jonny was sad. Not because he was losing the race but because he was lonely.

Am blockierten Tunnel war Jonny traurig. Nicht, weil er das Rennen verlor, sondern weil er einsam war.

Suddenly—sound of wheels. Those were Scott and Mike!

Plötzlich—das Geräusche von Rädern. Das waren Scott und Mike!

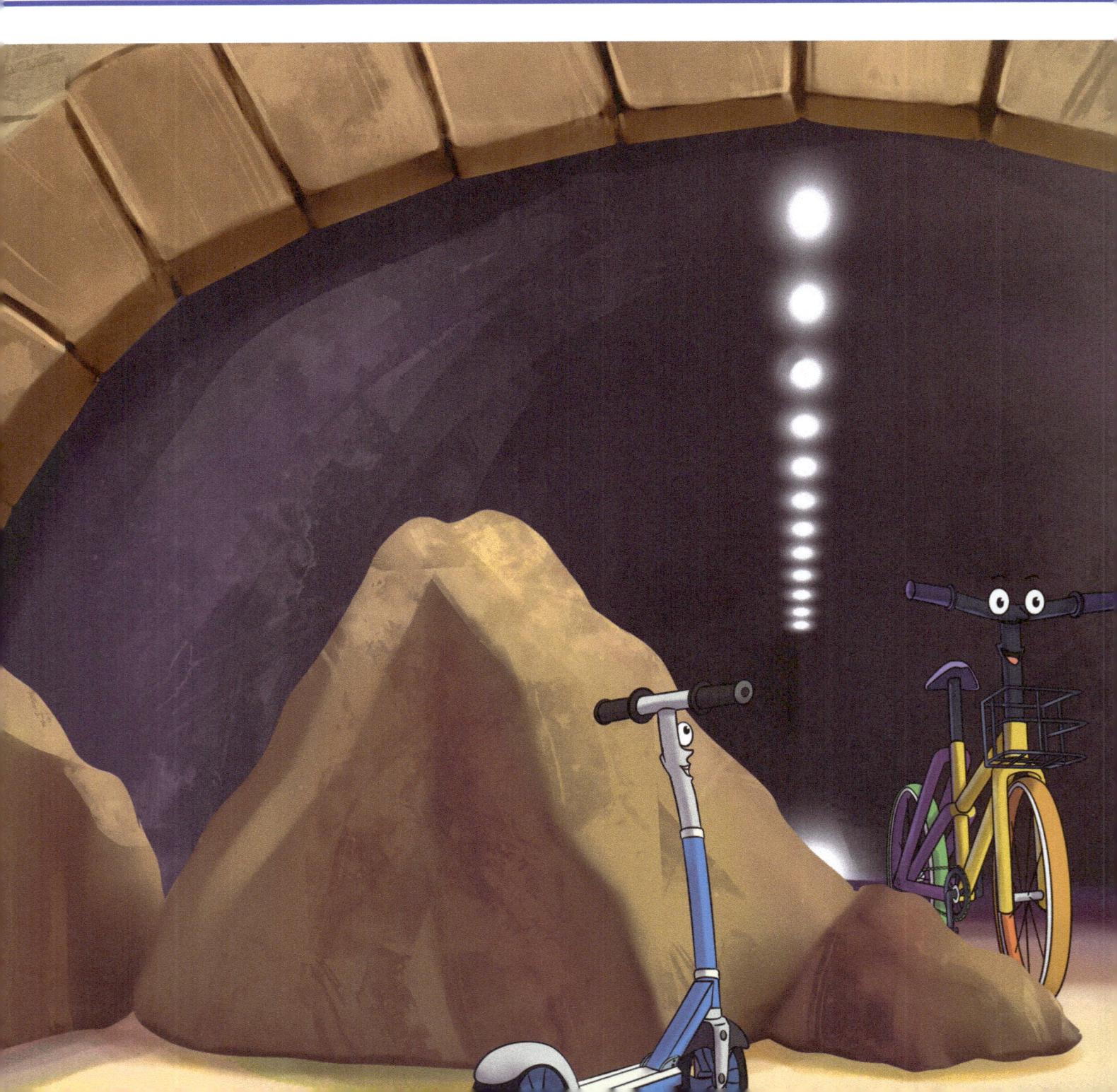

"Mike, Let's move these boulders so Jonny can pass," said Scott.

„Mike, lass uns die Felsbrocken wegschieben, damit Jonny durchfahren kann", sagte Scott.

The friends started to work together, pushing the rocks out of the way.

Die Freunde fingen an, gemeinsam zu arbeiten, und schoben die Felsen aus dem Weg.

It wasn't easy, but they nudged and nudged and soon there was enough space for Jonny to squeeze through.

Es war nicht einfach, doch sie schoben und schoben und bald war genug Platz, so dass Jonny sich durchzwängen konnte.

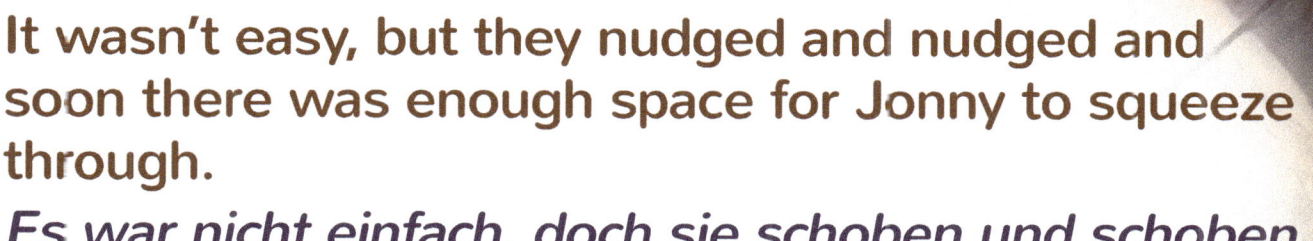

Giggling, they reached the end of Hill Road.
Kichernd erreichten sie das Ende der Hügelstraße.

"We've won the race—all of us!" exclaimed Mike and Scott.
„Wir haben das Rennen gewonnen—wir alle!", riefen Mike und Scott.

Only Jonny was quiet. "I behaved badly with you," he admitted. "I realized it late, guys that together we can do much more. Thank you, my friends, for helping me understand that!"

Nur Jonny war still. „Ich habe mich euch gegenüber schlecht benommen", gab er zu. „Ich habe es spät begriffen, Leute, dass wir gemeinsam viel mehr tun können. Danke, meine Freunde, dass ihr mir geholfen habt, das zu verstehen!"

Suddenly, there was applause, cheering for this wonderful bunch of three terrific friends...

Plötzlich gab es Applaus und Jubel für diese wunderbare Gruppe von drei tollen Freunden...

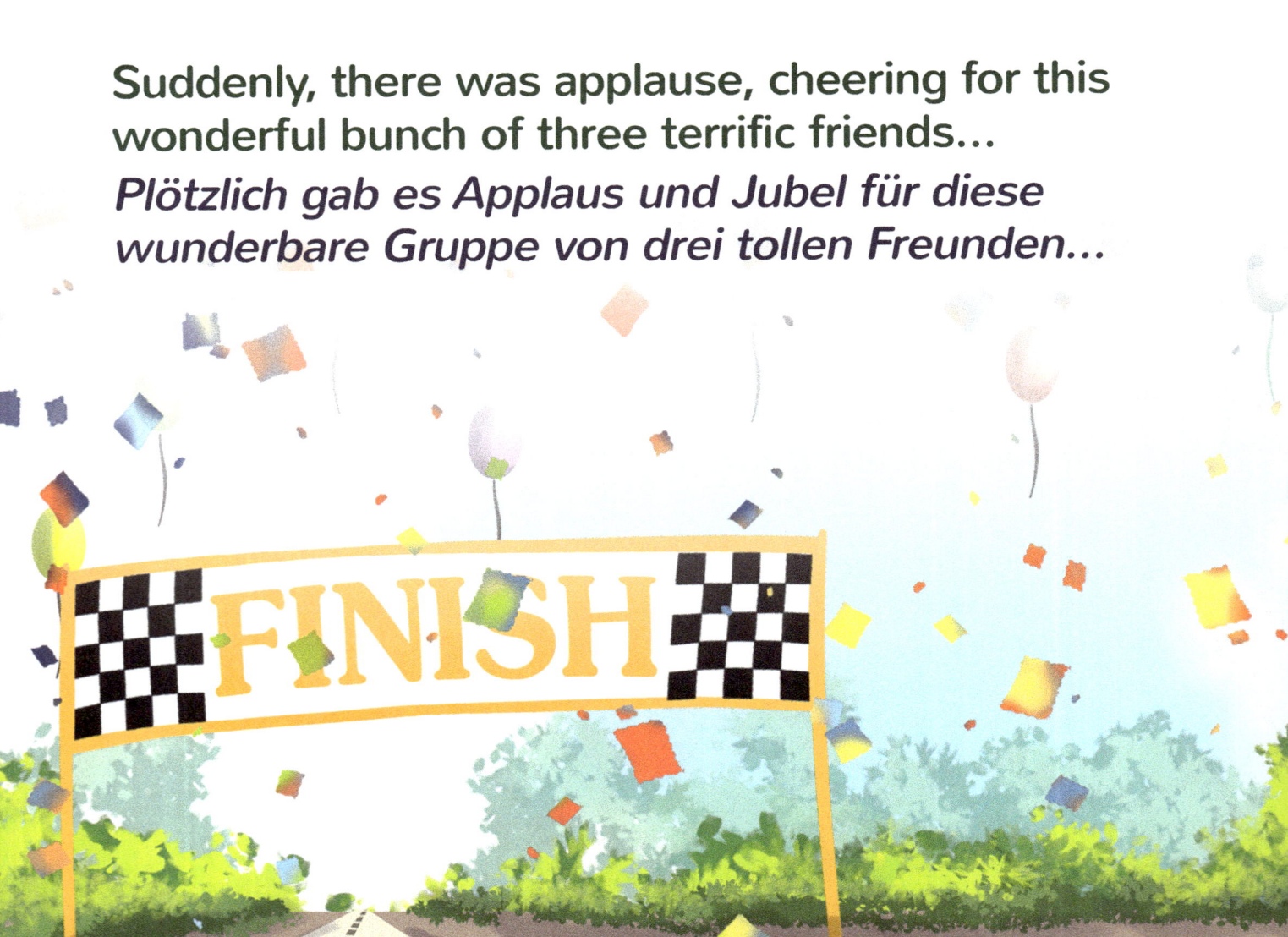

Friends who discovered that none of them was as good as all of them.

Freunde, die entdeckten, dass keiner von ihnen so gut war wie sie alle.

11.621 83820OLV00062B/4909 [4208264 72]

www.ingramcontent.com/pod-product-compliance
Lightning Source LLC
LaVergne TN